ACKNOWLEDGMENTS

Tommy Robinson- Daddy, I love you. I thank God he chose you to lead me, guide me, and teach me about the joys and pitfalls this life has to offer. Thank you for believing in me when I didn't believe in myself. Thank you for being an inspirational and motivating force in my life. You will always be the number one man in my life. I love you, daddy.

Alice Robinson- Mom, thank you for being you. It is through you I have learned patience, strength, and the power of prayer. I thank God He chose you to bring me into this world. Thank you for devoting your life to nurture and take care of me. I love you, mommy.

Karima Jamila Robinson- What a lively and vivacious spirit you have! Let it be known that without your love, support, and tenacious ways, I would not be where I am today. I have learned more from you (my younger sister) than you would believe. I love you for all you are and everything you are destined to be.

M'Lita Carr Gaither- Fate would not have it that we should be born into the same family; however, that has not stopped me from embracing you as my sister. Thank you for not allowing time and distance to separate us. Thank you for allowing me to be me without ever casting judgement. This is truly rare. You have always been there for me. For you, my love and devotion will never end. Thank you for being my best friend. I love you.

Marc Norwood- You have always sought truth. You are truly a God-fearing man. You do your best to walk upright in His eyes. I love you and respect you for all that you are and for the spirit that lives within you. I thank God for our friendship, for truly it is rare. Thank you for your contribution to this project and to my life. You never have to wonder about my love and devotion towards you. It will never end.

Narviar Calloway- You are truly a blessing. Thank you for your encouragement and support. There is a quiet and gentle yet soaring spirit that lies within you. I am grateful you chose to share parts of you with me. Thank you for believing in me.

Becky Butler- You are truly a God-send. You saved my life and for that I am truly grateful. Thank you for allowing the Spirit to guide you while you so generously opted to take this journey with me. Thank you. Thank you. Thank You. Who would have thought therapy could be so healing?!

Rod Hollimon- The crossing of our paths is not accidental, however a matter of fate and timing. Thank you for believing in my work and for believing in me. Together, I believe we will make a magnificent team. I could not have asked for a more dedicated publisher. Thank you for all of your support.

Within Your Reach

Inspiration that Quiets the Mind

&

Soothes the Soul

by

Monifa W. Robinson, MSW, MPA

Urban Thought Books
Atlanta, GA

Published in the USA by
Urban Thought Books
Atlanta, GA
www.urbanthoughtbooks.com

ISBN: 1-930231-03-2
LCCN: 2003110359
Book Layout & Cover Design: Rod Hollimon
Editor: Narviar C. Calloway, M.S.W., PH.D.

It is refreshing to know that in a world so chaotic, God has strategically placed individuals in my life who have deposited seeds of wisdom and encouragement into me. I thank all of you for your individual gifts of love and support:

William T. Baker, Cecile Barron-Morse, Kathy Blackshear, Daphne Blick-Washington, Angelita Colbert, Walter Dixon, Rosalind Edochie, Ricardo Freeman, Thomas Green, LaDonna Hightower, Gregory Jemison, Adrienne Johnson, Rita Lassiter, Ronnie Lassiter, Shena Leverett, Charles Lewis, Shawn Martin, Dana Myers, Lamarr Norris, Chauntwanette Okantey, Johnny Payne, Gerard Payne, Petrina Payne, Keith Perkins, Kayla Stevens, Regina F. Stevens, Camille Smith, Mary Solomon, Wendy Truitt,Crystal Wesley, Anthony Williams, WIR (Women In Recovery), Family and Friends.

Dedication

The Holy Trinity

God

You are the head of my life. Lord, you are the one who deposited this seed and uttered this prophetic calling into my life. Thank you. I will forever honor, bless, praise, and magnify your name.

Jesus Christ

Thank you for coming to earth in the form of a man to take on the sins of this world. You know my struggles. You are my strength. Ultimately, I look to you for tenacity to help me carry out the work God has set before me.

Holy Spirit

You have been a constant guide. You also have been my protector and my peace. For this I will forever be devoted and grateful.

TABLE OF CONTENTS

TOPICS

Reference: Biblical references/scriptures used are from the King James Version of the Bible and are credited and referenced appropriately.

Foreword

Absolutely inspiring, meaningful and significant to our daily lives, especially in today's times of chaos, war, trials and tribulations. These spiritual, yet challenging, passages written by Monifa Robinson are indeed uplifting and motivational. Her practical and candid scriptures are an inspiration to all of us as we move through our personal journeys in life. The simplistic message in each entry will awaken your inner soul and spirit.

As one intrinsically aware of the hardships and struggles that confront us in life, I have found the passages contained within this book to be soothing and insightful. I have found strength, solace and direction from these scriptures. Monifa gently, but realistically, captures the essence of faith, hope and direction as we let go... and let God...assist us in each of our exertions.

These passages are so timely today, as we seek the strength and courage to move forward, to commit to life, and to restore our faith in ourselves and in mankind. Thank you, Monifa, for your revelations.

Narviar C. Calloway, M.S.W., Ph.D.
Spelman College
Department of Psychology

LET THE HEALING BEGIN

*L*ife presents challenges that sometimes bring us to our highest level of vulnerability. However, what most people do not recognize is that they have inner strength even in their darkest moments of weakness. I write this book to be a servant to those in search of life's truest meaning. I want to provide others with the gift to go beyond themselves and to reach life's highest potential. I have defined potential as strength that reaches beyond the physical and transcends itself into the spiritual, which is what ultimately allows one to be truly fulfilled. In being a servant, I have found it necessary to first search my own being and seek the truth to purify my own soul. My Higher Power, whom I choose to call God, inspired the book you are about to read.

It was in the midst of a turbulent storm that I was *forced (given no option)* to let go, to listen and to trust in God. I know this may be hard for some readers to believe because the average person believes that personal choices are controlled. This, too, is what I thought until I came to a place in my life where the spirit held me still, for there was an important lesson for me to learn. There was a book for me to write. It was in this quiet place that this book was born. He (God) forced me to take inventory and begin the process of cleansing my own soul. God forced me to stop running away from myself, from my fears, and to accept my destiny. Only then was I to become fulfilled. God showed me how to search my heart, how to let go, and how to become his servant. In this place, though my tears, I opened my heart and soul to His spirit, and the words began to flow. A messenger was within me over which I no longer had control! I began a new journey that day. In those quiet moments with God, my eyes were lifted, definitions became clearer, and a little more light appeared to brighten my path. I emerged as a servant of God. It is amazing what will happen when you follow *His* plan for your life.

No one, not even I, will ever complete this journey, but this is not the point. I look at my life and recognize that no matter how horrible things appear to be at times, they always get better. I am not just speaking about the tangible. I am talking about everything. My character grows stronger; my patience and tolerance extend farther; and my understanding grows broader. I do not want to stop this journey. If I have come this far in such a short amount of time, then imagine what is in store for me as I continue forward? I know now that I want more of what God and the universe has to offer.

This meditation book represents my journey. This journey is about Thoughts, Emotions, Actions, Control *or lack thereof*, Issues, Truth, Dare, Choice, Obedience, Submission, Responsibility, Acceptance, Consequence, Faith, Patience, and most importantly, Honesty, which is where true healing begins.

There is so much more for me to share with you and even more for me to learn. Let this be the beginning.

My hope and prayer is that my journey will inspire you to begin your own healing process. The time has come. There is no time like the present. Why put off for tomorrow, what you can do today? Much work must be done in order to feel whole and complete. This is not to disillusion you. Although many trials may persist, your spirit, your perspective and your faith will help you make it through. I urge you to let the healing begin.

Honesty

This journey is about Honesty...which is where true healing begins.

Honesty

Definition: The ability to search for and act upon truth despite the consequences.

So, I say I want to heal my emotional wounds. I say I am tired of allowing my past experiences to bind me and keep me from reaching my fullest potential. Oh and by the way, did I tell you I am willing to do this at *any* cost?! Well the cost, my dear, is honesty. Seems easy enough, doesn't it. Bosh! Think again. If I remember nothing else, I must remember just one thing: *Honesty hurts before it heals.* In order to be honest with myself, I must unravel some deep dark secrets. I must stare my inconsistencies and vulnerabilities in the face. I must admit to myself that I am flawed; perhaps more flawed than I am willing or even able to deal with at this time. This is the first step I must take if I am to make a conscientious decision to travel the road that leads to healing. This one terrifying, antagonizing, and painful step is worth the freedom and peace it brings. Once I become honest with me, I automatically place myself in a position of power. Positive energy now has the ability to move through me. Positive people and positive things have no other option but to surround me. And then I will know that the healing has begun. There is no other way to travel along this road to be successful unless I take with me truth and honesty.

...whatsoever things are true,...and honest,...think on these things.

Philippians 4:8

How does honesty allow me to heal?

_____

_____

_____

_____

_____

_____

_____

_____

_____

_____

_____

_____

_____

_____

_____

_____

_____

_____

_____

_____

_____

_____

_____

_____

AWARENESS

Remember your situation could be worse.

*I*always think I have involved myself in the worst possible scenario. No one could possibly be in greater debt, have a more unhealthy relationship, or have experienced a greater loss than I. At least that is what I tell myself. God has news for me. I am wrong. The real problem is not what I experience but how I choose to experience my experience. I have a tendency to fall into the mode of self-pity. Once I fall into that mode of self-pity, I isolate myself and maximize the negative energy that swiftly surrounds and engulfs me instead of allowing positivity to enthrall and captivate me. Most times when I fall into this mode of self-pity, it is because I have become caught in a sadistic cycle with which I become comfortable. This cycle must be broken. Part of breaking this cycle is knowing that my problem is greater than me. It is knowing that I am simply being used for a purpose far greater than I can fathom. It is knowing that there is a spiritual purpose and answer to every earthly situation. It is knowing that I am not alone.

To every thing there is a season, and a time to every purpose under the heaven...
Ecclesiastes 3:1

Monifa Robinson

How can self-pity keep me from attaining my goals?

CONTENTMENT

I must be like Paul; I must learn to be content in whatever state or condition I am in.

*O*h how difficult it is to be content, satisfied and at peace when the moonlight is not shining in the evening, and its glare is not shimmering off the clear blue waters. Oh how challenging it is to smile and strut with my head held high when the night falls and the darkness is not only darkness, but has become a deep dark abyss whose mysteries have yet to unfold. It is during these crucial moments that I am reminded that I must be like Paul; I must learn to be content in whatever state or condition I am in.

It is imperative to my emotional well-being, spiritual growth, mental status and physical health, to be like Paul. For I know if I can learn to be like Paul, knowing that learning is a process and simply requires that I experience life situations, take a series of tests and pass, that the ultimate result is growth; and, my life would improve significantly. Isn't growth part of what life is all about anyway?! I can not grow if I can not employ the belief of Paul.

I have learned, in whatsoever state I am, therewith to be content.
Philippians 4:11

How can I become more content in my personal journey?

_____
_____
_____
_____
_____
_____
_____
_____
_____
_____
_____
_____
_____
_____
_____
_____
_____
_____
_____
_____
_____
_____
_____
_____
_____
_____

DISCOURAGED

When you feel down, look up.

There is something about the physical act of looking up. No matter how bad the situation, looking up tends to release burdens and alleviate stress. It is a sign that no matter how hopeless I feel, the subconscious believes that possibilities do exist. There is the belief that although results can not be seen, there **is** going to be a brighter day. When I feel down, I always look up.

I will lift up mine eyes unto the hills, from whence cometh my

help.

Psalms 121:1

How can lifting my eyes bring me strength?

Don't be discouraged.

Discouraged

Definition: Persuaded by person or circumstance to repress your vision and lose hope.

Walking in purpose is like walking a tight rope with a trampoline underneath me. If I am not careful and do not remain focused, it is easy to become distracted. The good thing is, if I fall off the tight rope I fall onto the trampoline, which helps me bounce back. It is amazing how many things come my way to discourage me and redirect me from the path I am destined to follow. If I am not careful, I will allow people and circumstance to discourage me and to persuade me to lose sight of my vision and purpose. In order to remain focused, prayer and meditation must become as routine as saying thank you, yet not as ritualistic as brushing my teeth. For once it becomes ritualistic, the true meaning is lost. Remember, don't be discouraged. Don't allow person or circumstance to repress my vision and cause me to lose hope.

Fear not, nor be dismayed, be strong and of good courage...
Joshua 10:25

How can I encourage myself when I become discouraged?

_____

_____

_____

_____

_____

_____

_____

_____

_____

_____

_____

_____

_____

_____

I thought God was disappointed in me because I was depressed, discouraged, and distressed, but a good friend reminded me of God's grace.

I am so thankful that Jesus came to earth. Oh, how wonderful it is to know that he really does understand the problems I encounter. However, I am not always this confident. When challenges come, sometimes I tend to forget that God really does understand and forgives. Whenever I become depressed, discouraged, and distressed I am not exercising faith. Fear becomes the driving and motivating force behind which all decisions are made. How happy could God be with me when I react with fear versus faith? This is the question I ask myself. I realize that to disappoint friends, family, and loved ones is one thing, but to feel as though I have disappointed the One who is truly the author of "life" is no comparison. I thank God for His love, patience and mercy. I thank Him for not giving up on me.

And he said unto me, My Grace is sufficient for thee: for my strength is made perfect in weakness.

II Corinthians 12:9

How has God's grace prevailed in my life?

_____

_____

_____

_____

_____

_____

_____

_____

_____

_____

_____

_____

_____

_____

_____

_____

_____

_____

ENCOURAGEMENT

I need encouragement too.

*E*nough Said.

> *Help me, O Lord my God...*
> *Psalm 109:26*

How will I encourage myself?

FAITHFULNESS

I must first prove myself faithful.

So often I develop feelings of jealously and anger because I see others relishing in extraordinary and peculiar blessings. I begin to question why someone else has so "much" and I have so "little." I want great things, but the problem is I don't want to take on the tasks required to attain greatness. I want that pot of gold at the end of the rainbow, but it slips my mind that this pot of gold is actually at the end of the rainbow, and, that prior to the delightful rainbow that appears, is usually a tumultuous storm. This is the type of storm that awakens me at night, not allowing me to rest peacefully. Many times I want to be rich but I am not mature enough to handle the "mediocre" salary I currently receive. I want to live in a 5-bedroom home, but complain about keeping my one bedroom apartment clean. I must understand that loyalty, commitment, dedication and discipline do not come easy, but are considered necessary modes of transportation to arriving at greater things. So when I begin to want more, I should check myself to see if I have proven myself faithful where I stand.

A faithful man shall abound with blessings:...

Proverbs 28:20

I remember when I remained faithful, and as a result, received "my" reward.

_____

_____

_____

_____

_____

_____

_____

_____

_____

_____

_____

_____

_____

_____

_____

_____

FEAR

Lord, I apologize for any fear and doubt I have allowed myself to experience.

*T*he key word here is "allowed". This term implies permission· When I allow fear and doubt to engulf me, I am voluntarily giving these feelings permission to settle in my spirit. Lord, please accept my sincerest apology. I know you have not given me the spirit of fear. Sometimes fear and doubt cause me to miss out on opportunities and blessings. These very feelings can immobilize me and place me in positions that inevitably prohibit my growth. However, I must remember that although YOU are a forgiving God and that YOU will accept my apologies, I must begin to change my behavior so that my requests for forgiveness decrease in this area.

For God hath not given us the spirit of fear; but of power, and of love, and of a sound mind.
II Timothy 1:7

How do fear and doubt hinder my journey?

_____

_____

_____

_____

_____

_____

_____

_____

_____

_____

_____

_____

_____

_____

_____

JOY

It is true; Joy does come in the morning. I am a witness!

*D*espite the darkness, there is a light at the end of the tunnel. There is a pot of gold on the other side of the rainbow. The problem is, I usually don't want to endure the thunderstorms, strong winds, and tornadoes. I just want to marvel at the rainbow in the sky and bask in the warmth of the sun. Oh, but I am sorry to know that the rainbow is never evident unless there has been some rain. Hold on! Don't I know that the darkest part of the night is just before the break of day? Look at how much strength I possess. Only a person as strong as me would be able to hold on this long. When I know that the sun is going to come up, I don't worry about the rain. Why? Because I know that this, too, shall pass. I will simply put on my raincoat and galoshes for protection and trudge through the mud knowing that it is true, joy does come in the morning.

Weeping may endure for a night, but joy cometh in the morning.
Psalm 30:5

I do remember a time when I had a "breakthrough" just before I was about to give up.

_____

_____

_____

_____

_____

_____

_____

_____

_____

_____

_____

_____

_____

_____

_____

_____

PAIN

I may not complain, but I am human too, I also feel pain.

*H*ave you ever been around a constant complainer? Well, if you have, you know the energy they bring is negative and can prey upon your spirit. If you are already agitated, the complainer exacerbates the problem and if you are at peace, it can begin to stir up some feelings of irritability. Either way you don't feel good around a complainer. I have chosen not to become a complainer.

Question: Does this mean I don't have my challenges?

Answer: Of course not.

Question: Does this mean I am not true to my feelings and myself?

Answer: No.

I choose to utilize specific external resources and draw from my internal resources to resolve my difficulties as effectively as I can. I usually have more internal resources than I give myself credit for. By the time adulthood is reached, I prove myself to be a survivor. I shall tap into the strength that brought me this far. I will find that once I do this, I will complain less. I will then watch others become baffled and wonder if I ever experience pain. At this point, I will then be able to say, "I may not complain, but I am human, too; I also feel pain."

We, then, that are strong ought to bear the infirmities of the weak.

Romans 15:1

How does complaining affect me and others around me?

_____

_____

_____

_____

_____

_____

_____

_____

_____

_____

_____

_____

_____

_____

_____

PATIENCE

My time will come when my time comes

So often I look at others as they enjoy their blessings and wonder when will I receive my blessing? When will my change come? When will I be able to experience the fruits of my labor? Well, the answer is simple. When it's my time. What I must understand is that time is relative. My schedule and time line are most often inaccurate. Does this mean I should not plan and set goals? Of course not. However, I do not need to follow and set my sites and goals on what others have. I need to be in tune with my own spirit. My spirit will provide guidance and will inform me of the pace I am to move. When I do this, I can say with blessed assurance that my time will come when my time comes.

Humble yourselves therefore under the mighty hand of God, that He may exalt you in due time.

I Peter 5:6

What can I do while I'm waiting for my time to come?

_____

_____

_____

_____

_____

_____

_____

_____

_____

_____

_____

_____

_____

_____

_____

_____

Patience

Definition: Calm Endurance

*I*t appears to me that patience and faith work hand in hand. I cannot endure any situation with calmness if I do not have hope and believe that regardless of the end result, things ultimately work out right. When I have done all that I can do and I allow the universe to do the rest, it then becomes easy to wait and endure. Waiting with patience does not imply that action stops. It simply implies that I have an awareness and confidence that whatever will be, will be. When I understand the true underlying meaning of patience, I understand that patience builds character, which is what really matters anyway. Patience.

For ye have need of patience, that, after ye have done the will of God, ye might receive the promise.

Hebrews 10:36

How being more patient affects my physical, mental, and spiritual well-being?

PRAISE

Praise is pertinent.

I must remember that when I show thanks and appreciation, my situation appears a little brighter; that is because the object of praise is to uplift. I take my mind off of the "process" (problem) and allow myself to focus on the positive things the universe has to offer me. It helps me focus on personal growth and that which is pertinent, with praise.

Let us offer up the sacrifice of praise to God continually,...

Hebrews 13:15

If I decrease the number of complaints and increase the amount of praise, how will my life change?

PRAYER

Pray without ceasing.

*P*rayer is my connection. It is my life line; my oxygen tank. It is a process in which I learn to surrender my will and admit that without "Him" I am powerless and that I am nothing. Prayer does not always entail "asking." Neither does it require whaling, moaning and groaning for 60 minutes or more. Prayer does not require that all activities that help me gain momentum towards a higher goal cease. Prayer can be as simple as "Thank you," "Order my steps," or "Give me wisdom," uttered from the depths of my soul. Or it can be a time when I am still and allow room for positive energy to flow within me. I must not ever stop. I must keep moving. When I get tired and feel like giving up, I will pray. Prayer is a process in which a connection is developed. Pray without ceasing. It works.

Pray without ceasing.

I Thessalonians 5:17

What will I do differently with my prayer life?

_____

_____

_____

_____

_____

_____

_____

_____

_____

_____

_____

_____

_____

_____

_____

_____

PROCESS

Don't focus on the process. Focus on the product.

*D*on't underestimate the power of energy. Energy, depending on how it is used, can exacerbate and drain or it can elevate and motivate. As a result, it is extremely "precious" and needs to be employed wisely. Process is a method or procedure in which energy is required in order to reach a goal. Process is rarely pleasant and often painful. Process normally entails being taken out of my element and comfort zone and being placed in a situation that forces me to extend and enlarge myself to get the job done. If I focus and obsess over what needs to be done to reach the end result, more than likely, I will end up miserable. However if I keep my eye on the prize, I will more often than not remain motivated to keep pushing forward. I must remember how wonderful it is when I reach my goal. Don't focus on the process; focus on the product.

This one thing I do, forgetting those things which are behind,
and reaching forth unto those things which are before, I press
toward the prize...
Philippians 3:13-14

How can I stay motivated when problems arise?

SELF-PITY

When I know His (God's) word, I know nothing happens by accident.

When I know His word, not when I have heard it. Not when I have memorized it, not when I can look up themes in the Concordance of the Bible, Not when I remember what others told me, but when I have developed a relationship with God, when I have a deep sense of comfort, when I have prayed and meditated and followed God's word and asked for clarity, it is only then that I am unmoved, centered, and sure that nothing in my life occurs as a result of coincidence. Nothing is ironic. Nothing is accidental. It is at this pivotal moment that I am at peace. The sleepless nights I have are minimal, my stress level decreases and the cares of life do not weigh down upon my shoulders like a heavy boulder. This process does not come easy. It does require an incredible amount of trust. Not trust in myself and what I think I can do, but trust in a being greater than the human mind can imagine. Without this type of trust and faith, it is impossible to experience this type of serenity. I constantly remind myself that when I know His (God's) word, I know nothing happens by accident.

And they that know thy name will put their trust in thee: for thou, Lord, hast not forsaken them that seek thee.

Psalm 9:10

How can establishing a relationship with God alter my perspective on life?

STRENGTH

Yes, I have an incredible amount of strength, but do you know what I had to go through to get it?

*T*here seems to be this grand misconception that individuals with astronomical amounts of strength, stamina and wisdom have it goin' on all the time. Oh contraire! These are people who have toiled and paced the floors in the midnight hour, picked up the phone to call someone for help, only to receive voicemail. These individuals are admired by others because they have a smile on their face, but others have no idea that their eyes swelled shut from tears cried just the night before, and migraine medication was taken to assist in relieving some frontal lobe pressure. Others have no idea that prayer and meditation are at the forefront and no matter how difficult, it is practiced with a certain level of consistency and sincerity. Everyone wants what I have. If only they knew I still have such a long way to go. Does this mean they should not strive to get to this level? No, of course not, but it is imperative for them to know that without pain, there is no gain. Yes, I have an incredible amount of strength, but do you know what I had to go through to get it?

No weapon that is formed against thee shall prosper;...

Isaiah 54:17

I recall 3 life altering events that brought me to a higher level in life.

_____

_____

_____

_____

_____

_____

_____

_____

_____

_____

_____

_____

_____

_____

_____

_____

_____

Allow me to be me. Allow me to be both strong and weak.

*T*here is no feeling worse than the one of a good friend or family member who won't <u>allow</u> me to be me. I remember a time when I thought I was talking to a 'friend' about some painful issues. During our conversation tears of sorrow began to run down my cinnamon brown cheeks. The next thing I heard him say was "NO NOT YOU", (referring to my state of sadness, evidenced by tears). I immediately became angry and reminded him I, too, am human. Enraged, I could do nothing except clam up and think about how my "friend" really didn't know me. The pain of this experience was enough for me to make one request of all I meet. From now on, my request is simple: *Allow me to be me. Allow me to be both strong and weak.*

Let the words of my mouth, and the meditation of my heart, be acceptable in thy sight,...
Psalm 19:14

How do I learn from both my strengths and my weaknesses?

THANKFULNESS

I am truly thankful.

*B*eing thankful is a lifestyle. It is a way of being. Thankfulness does not only manifest itself through verbal expression. It emanates through my very being. The way I treat myself and others shows my level of gratitude. When I am thankful for something or for someone, I nurture that thing; I foster an attitude of gracefulness. "TLC" (Tender Loving Care) no longer becomes a cliché but is now reality. How can I say I am truly thankful for life when I feed my body poison? How can I say I am thankful for money when I do not respect it and use it unwisely? Thankfulness is not a result of pressure or guilt, and does not operate out of fear. True thankfulness is a result of knowing that each moment is a gift. I am truly thankful.

A gift is a precious stone in the eyes of him that hath it:...

Proverbs 17:8

Ten ways I will show more gratitude:

_____

_____

_____

_____

_____

_____

_____

_____

_____

_____

_____

_____

_____

_____

Faith

My faith can take me anywhere I want to go.

*A*nywhere? Now wait a minute. Does this mean there is no limit? Surely I must be understating the truth when I say anywhere. Well, I guess I can think of it this way. What other options do I have? I can believe the opposite, but what good will that do? Well, I choose to believe in the power of faith. I strongly believe my faith can help me climb the highest mountain; it can help me swim the deepest sea; it can change my situation in the midnight hour. I am a witness that faith can see me through my darkest night. Often times, my fears have a tendency to become my reality, which pushes my faith to the back burner. This causes me to believe the "impossible" truly is impossible. If there is one thing I have learned about faith, it is this: *faith is about the "impossible."* Otherwise what good is it?! Faith is a mechanism God uses to get me to rely on Him. When I exercise faith, I reach beyond myself and the power I have, and I rely on a force greater than myself to complete the task. The reason faith works is because it goes beyond me and you and what the human eye can see. I am convinced. My faith can take me anywhere I want to go.

If ye have faith...ye shall say unto the mountain move, and it shall move; and nothing shall be impossible unto you.

Matthew 17:20

What will I do to strengthen my faith?

_____

_____

_____

_____

_____

_____

_____

_____

_____

_____

_____

_____

_____

_____

_____

Guidance

Wow, my steps are truly ordered by the Lord!

*I*t is so amazing, mind blowing, astonishing, miraculous, and awesome. Need I go on?! And all this time I thought I had no purpose. All this time I thought my life was nothing more than chaotic. At best an "organized mess", whatever that really means. All this time I was depressed and thought my life was nothing but rubbish, not even suited for the finest junkyard. Hmm, but when I take a moment to sit back and take inventory and review my own history, I realize there is some method to this madness. I could not see it at every stage, but His track record has been perfect all along. It was spotless. It was impeccable. He never made a mistake. I started wondering, why was it that I could not see His marvelous works? Was it because I was so focused on me? Was I so focused on my problems that my *vision* became blurred? Was I too busy complaining? Whatever the reason, I now know there is a rainbow after every storm. I have more respect and reverence for my Father above. I now have more faith in the Man who has mapped out my life and navigated me through the rough terrain. I am not only amazed, but I am truly thankful. My steps are truly ordered by the Lord.

The steps of a good man are ordered by the Lord.
Psalm 37:23

When did I realize my steps were ordered by the lord?

_____

_____

_____

_____

_____

_____

_____

_____

_____

_____

_____

_____

_____

_____

_____

_____

How do I know? My spirit tells me so.

*H*ow do I know I am making the right decision? How do I know I have chosen the right path? How do I know I am not headed toward destruction? I know when I have peace. I know when my spirit is at ease. I know these things and I can be sure when I have released myself from the situation; when I have relinquished control. There is a calmness and a sense of resolve when the right move has been made. I must however remain centered. I must stay connected to my Higher Power. I must be careful not to allow me to get in the way. His way will be the only way I will know. His way is the only way I can be sure. Whenever I need to know, I can rest assured that if I am still, my spirit will tell me so.

For God is not the author of confusion, but of peace...

I Corinthians 14:33

How will I listen to my spirit?

Purpose

I will not allow my past to dictate my future

*T*he key word is "allow". This is a simple yet subtly pungent word. I will not give my past *permission* to shadow over me and create a world where I feel doom is inevitable. As challenging as it may be, I am determined to reach my potential. I am determined to move beyond past hurts and pain. I am determined to move above and beyond my wildest dreams. I am determined to create a new me. In order to do this, I must be willing to let go of some things. I must be prepared to travel this road alone. I must understand that everyone will not accompany me as I reach higher heights in my journey. I must find a healthy way to deal with my hurt and pain. This is the only way my future will be different from my past. This is the only way I will move closer to my purpose.

...old things are passed away; behold all things are become new.

II Corinthians 5:17

How can walking with honesty and integrity effect my future?

_____

_____

_____

_____

_____

_____

_____

_____

_____

_____

_____

_____

_____

_____

_____

_____

_____

_____

Walk with purpose and you will walk into your destiny.

Destiny

Definition: pre-ordained future.

*L*et every step I take and every decision I make be carried out with precision. Let there be order. Let there be confidence. Let there be intent. It is amazing what is laid before me when I am focused; when I put pride into everything I do. Not the type of pride that allows me to set myself above the rest, but the type of pride that allows me to walk with my head held high while i still have humility in my heart. You see, I believe, the steps I take are a precursor to my future. Even if I am not sure of what my future holds, I am convinced that if I walk with a sense of integrity and honesty, purpose is bound to meet me somewhere on my journey and take me to my destiny.

*...**as for me, I will walk in mine integrity**...*

Psalms 26:11

What is my divine purpose?

Free Will

Get yourself together, but don't leave ME out of the process.

*I*t is His desire that I get myself together; that I move along the path He has chosen for me; that I follow His way. It is His will that I reach higher heights. It is His will that I expand my mind; that I open my heart; that I unstop my ears. But He begs and pleads with me not to forget Him. He wants so desperately to be an integral part of my life. He also wants me to realize that the only way I can truly get myself together is to develop a personal relationship with Him. If I do this, success is my only option. If I join myself to Him, His word, and His ways, He will make a covenant (promise) to give me the desire of my heart. But the amazing thing about it is He doesn't force me. He gives me free will. Life would be so much easier if I would just give Him permission to join me as I attempt to correct the wrongs in my life. It is true. When I think about the times I did let Him in, I was at peace. I felt a sense of comfort. Although trouble was on every side, somehow I felt I could go on. There was something to live for. Now when I think about the times when I took "free will" and did with it what I wanted, I remember there was nothing but chaos. I have made my decision. I would rather have peace, so Lord please join me as I go through this process.

...let us join ourselves to the Lord...
Jeremiah 50:5

How is my life different when I let God be a part of the process?

_____

_____

_____

_____

_____

_____

_____

_____

_____

_____

_____

_____

_____

_____

_____

_____

_____

_____

_____

I can be your guide, only if you let me.

*I*sn't God wonderful?! He won't force Himself upon me. He gives me free will. He gives me the freedom to choose. How awesome! However, sometimes I, as a human, do not do well with too many options. Sometimes I take the scenic route to get to my destination, when I could have taken a more direct path. Then I wonder why my journey seems so drawn out. If only I would request a guided tour. Things would be in order and I could probably benefit a lot more if I would allow Him to guide me. The blessings are plentiful when I follow Him and the path He has set before me.

...the Lord shall guide thee continually, and satisfy thy soul...and thou shalt be like a watered garden, and like a spring of water, whose waters fail not.

Isaiah 58:11

What are the benefits of God being my guide?

Perserverance

Some will stay and some will go, either way I must continue.

*O*h this journey can sometimes be joyous and at other times it can be heart wrenching. One thing I have realized is that everyone is not meant to travel this path with me. I have learned to accept that someone I love and care for deeply can be there for me in the beginning -- with their course destined to change at any given point in *my* race. It is during these times that I must remember to be thankful, reflect on the good times and continue to move forward. If I do not, I put myself at risk of remaining stagnant. I may spend my time and energy fighting battles I was never meant to fight; focusing on enemies with whom I need not concern myself, and loose sight of my vision. The problem however, is that sometimes it is hard to let go of what I am so familiar with despite the pain and discomfort that often times accompanies me. In order for me to advance, I must realize and accept the fact that some will stay and some will go, either way I must continue.

...let us lay aside every weight and let us run the race that is set before us...

Hebrews 12:1

What must I let go of in order to move forward in my journey?

Vision

Just open your eyes and you will see the light.

So often the answer is right in front of me and I will see it if I just open my eyes. The answer isn't usually one that requires complex calculations. Neither does it require in-depth psychoanalytic therapy. The answer is usually clear. It is my emotions that get in the way and cause me to complicate matters. It doesn't take a rocket scientist. The answer is simple; just open my eyes.

Thy word is a lamp unto my feet and a light unto my path.

Psalm 119:105

**How do my emotions cloud my vision and cause me to be con-
fused and uncentered?**

Protection

He keeps blessing me!!!!!!

*H*e keeps on blessing me. He has angels watching over me. Each day He gives me brand new mercy. Thank you Lord for looking out for me! When I think of how YOU bless me, the way YOU constantly place YOUR shield of protection around me, I can't help but lift my hands, sing a song, and do a dance. I can not ever begin to pay YOU for YOUR mercy and the way YOU keep me safe from harm. Without YOUR mercy and YOUR grace, I know that I can not make it down here in this place we call earth. YOUR angels are strategically encamped around me to keep me protected from all danger, seen and unseen. Sometimes I sit and I am amazed, sometimes I am walking around in a daze, in wonderment over the things YOU have given me and how YOU have so graciously led me into my destiny. All I can say is YOU keep blessing me and I love it!!!!!!

And all these blessing shall come on thee, and overtake thee,...blessed shalt thou be in the city,...in the field,...when thou come...and when thou go...The Lord shall open unto thee His good treasure...Deuteronomy 28:2-13

Five blessings that God has bestowed upon me are:

_____

_____

_____

_____

_____

_____

_____

_____

_____

_____

_____

_____

_____

_____

_____

_____

_____

_____

_____

_____

_____

Whatever your desire- Whatever your dream-It's all within your reach

*T*he key word in this phrase is "all". Not some; not most; not a significant amount; not a portion; but, "ALL". I once heard a minister say, God doesn't give you a vision without making provision. This statement is extremely powerful and true. I should never think my dreams are too far fetched. I should never let the flame die. I should do everything in my power to keep the fire burning. This means I must work diligently until my time comes. If I can conceive the idea, I must believe I am capable of carrying this idea full term. During this incubation period, I must not get weary. I must not give up. I must do all the necessary things to see my dreams come to pass. When I do my part, God will make good on His promise and do the rest.

...the desire of the righteous shall be granted.

Proverbs 10:24

What do I want and how do I obtain it?

About the Author

Monifa Robinson, a native of New York City, moved to Teaneck, New Jersey with her family at the tender age of twelve. Upon graduation from Teaneck High School, Robinson obtained a Bachelor of Arts Degree in Psychology from Clark Atlanta University as well as a Masters of Social Work Degree from Smith College School of Social Work in Northampton, Massachusetts. After relocating to Atlanta, Georgia, and extensive work in the field of social services, she obtained a Masters of Public Administration Degree with a concentration in Management from Troy State University.

Monifa Robinson has devoted her life to helping others see the potential that lies within. That lifelong social devotion is the engine that drives her to continue providing services to diverse populations - including psychiatric patients, victims and predators of sexual cruelty, substance abusers, and more recently in the criminal justice system as a Psychological Services Specialist. Her experience has taught her that neither position nor status dictates the level of pain and misfortune one may encounter. Her formal education, combined with intense work experience, has played a vital role in the work that she does today.

To book Monifa Robinson for book signings, contact the following:

Urban Thought Books, Inc.
Public Relations Department
P.O.Box 78306
Atlanta, GA 30357
pr@urbanthoughtbooks.com
404.668.0940

To book Monifa Robinson for interviews and/or special appearances, contact the following:

Within Your Reach Consulting Service
P.O. Box 724943
Atlanta, GA 31139
Publicrelations@withinyourreach.org
770.956.0043

For additional inspiration and information about Monifa Robinson, lon onto
www.withinyourreach.org

Whatever Your Desire - Whatever Your Dream - It's All...Within Your Reach

We want to know what you think about this book. Please send praise and/or criticism, to the following:

readercomments@urbanthoughtbooks.com

or

P.O. Box 78306
Atlanta GA 30357

Urban Thought Books, Inc.
empowering writers, enlightening minds

www.urbanthoughtbooks.com

www.ingramcontent.com/pod-product-compliance
Lightning Source LLC
Chambersburg PA
CBHW051817040426
42446CB00007B/712